Trudy Matoody

By Marcia Ashford

Illustrated by Sergio Drumond

Copyright 2018 Heartstring Productions, LLC
Published and Distributed in the United States by: Marcia McGee Ashford

Trudy Matoody by Marcia McGee Ashford
Book Design and Supplemental Illustrations: Sergio Drumond

All rights reserved. No part of this publication may be reproduced, distributed, or transmitted in any form or by any means, including photocopying, recording, or other electronic or mechanical methods without the prior written permission of the publisher, except in the case of brief quotations embodied in critical reviews and certain other noncommercial uses permitted by copyright law.

Dedicated to My Mother

Mary Opal McGee

the Wind Beneath My Wings

Trudy Matoody was so excited! The rain had finally stopped, and she could go outside and walk down to the pond. Maybe she could find a new friend or two, even better, a friend who loves to sing!

She opened the front door and started to sing a happy song. Her beautiful voice attracted animals from all over the forest. They came closer and listened carefully until Trudy finished.

"I wish I could sing like you," said a grumpy looking frog sitting on a big, mossy rock. "My name is Bully Bullfrog, my dear. All I can do is Croak! Croak! Ribbety-Croak!"

As he sang the color green came floating from his quivering throat.

Green like grass and leaves in the spring. Green like lily pads!

The tiny ladybug sitting on a nearby tree limb laughed. "Gee Bully, at least you can sing. All I can get out is a hum." She let out a hum that was as quiet as a spring rain and had tones of red in it, "Ah-hum, ah-hum, ah-hummm."

Red like apples, and strawberries. Red like cherries!

She introduced herself. "I'm Jessica Ladybug, I love to hum and would like a new friend." Bully nodded his head in agreement. Trudy smiled a great big smile! She had two new friends!

They decided to go down to the pond together.
All three sang as they walked.
There was Trudy's beautiful voice.
Bully's Croak! Croak! Ribbety-Croak!
And Jessica's gentle Ah-hum, ah-hum,
ah-hummm

They heard a loud, unusual noise. "Lah, lah, meow, lah, meow."
"What is that?" asked Trudy.
"I don't know," said Jessica Ladybug. "But it sure sounds blue."
"Blue?" complained Bully. "Geez, I'd be blue too if my singing sounded like that!"

"Hush," Trudy and Jessica whispered in unison, "It might hear you and get its feelings hurt."

Slowly they tiptoed closer to the wailing sound coming out of a patch of cattails.

"Meow, meow, lah lah lah," sang the voice. "I am so blue, so blue, soo very, very blue."

"Hello," called Trudy. "Who are you and why are you so blue?"

Out popped a big, blue head with two green eyes and whiskers on either side of a tiny pink button nose.

"Lah, lah, meow, I am so blue because I have no friends," said the furry creature, as her tail swished back and forth into the tall stalks.

Her voice was blue like the sky and ocean waves. Blue like bluebirds and blueberries!

"Well, I am Trudy Matoody, and these are my new friends Bully Bullfrog and Jessica Ladybug," she said with confidence. "We would be happy to be your friends!"

"I am Kitty Kate," said the happy tabby. "What I wanted more than anything else was a friend and now I have three!" She bounced in dizzy circles all around her new friends, softly purring.

On to the pond they headed.
They sang as they walked.
You could hear...
Trudy's beautiful voice,
Shades of green: Croak! Croak! Ribbety-Croak!
Red: Ah-hum, ah-hum, ah-hummm
And blue: Lah, lah, meow, lah meow, lah, lah, meow, lah meow

"Hey, look!" shouted Trudy as she suddenly stopped and pointed at the nearby stream. "There is something under that lily pad. Isn't that your home, Bully Bullfrog?"

"Grump, ga-ga-lah grump, Croo-ak!" stuttered the frog. "Who dares to be in my home? Speak now or I will slime all over you!"

"Swish, swish, swishety-swish. I'm sorry," said a timid little fish.

She swam over to the friends and extended her shiny orange fin to Bully Bullfrog and the others. "My name is Gloria Goldfish."

She sang orange. You know orange like pumpkins and carrots. Orange like the fruit!

"Sorry to have bothered you. I didn't know this lily pad was taken. I was looking for a place to rest and maybe even find a friend or two."

"So be ours," sang out Trudy, with a big smile on her face. "We can always use another friend, right?" she asked, looking at her companions. They all nodded in agreement.

And on to the pond they headed.

They sang as they walked.

You could hear...

Trudy's beautiful voice,

Shades of green: Croak! Croak! Ribbety-Croak! Croak! Croak, Ribbety-Croak!

Red: Ah-hum, ah-hum, ah-hummm

Blue: Lah, lah, meow, lah meow, lah, lah, meow, lah meow

And orange: Swish, swishety-swish.

"Will you look at that!" yelled out a yellow butterfly sitting on a nearby rosebush.

"They sing in color!

Green like lily pads,

Red like cherries,

Blue like bluebirds,

And orange like oranges!"

"Flutter, flutter, flutter-by!" exclaimed his wife, Pinkey Purple Putterfly. "It looks like they are having so much fun. I wonder if they could use a couple of new friends?

We could add some more colors to their song." "We could add yellow, like the sun, pink and purple like spring flowers and Easter eggs!" exclaimed her excited husband, Yeller Putterfly. "Colors like you and me! Let's see if they have room for us!"

"Flutter, flutter, flutter-by. I thought you would never ask!" She smiled as they prepared for flight. Down they flitted and floated until they landed on the soft green grass close to the group.

When their song ended, Mr. Yeller Putterfly introduced himself and his wife, Pinkey Purple. "Pardon me, but we could not help hearing your beautiful song and would like to be a part of it. Could you use a couple of new friends?"

Trudy couldn't believe it! When she left home that afternoon, she just wanted to walk to the pond and possibly make a friend or two. Now she had so many new friends! There was Bully Bullfrog, Jessica Ladybug, Kitty Kate, and Gloria Goldfish.

Off they went on to the pond and into the setting sun:

Singing, laughing,
Laughing and singing,

Singing, laughing,
Laughing and singing some more!
Sometimes together,
Sometimes one at a time.

Their song was full of Trudy's beautiful voice,

Green: Croak! Croak! Ribbety-Croak!

Red: Ah-hum, ah-hum, ah-hummm

Blue: Lah, lah, meow, lah meow

Orange: Swish, swish, swishety-swish

With pink, purple and yellow: Flutter, flutter, flutter-by

www.ingramcontent.com/pod-product-compliance
Lightning Source LLC
Chambersburg PA
CBHW040736150426
42811CB00063B/1678